The Creation Seri
A Bible-based Reac

Animals

Carole Leah
and Sharon Rentta

NOTE TO PARENTS AND TEACHERS

The Creation Series consists of eight books based on the Genesis account in the Bible. This is the sixth book of this series and has been written from a Christian viewpoint. It is intended to be read *to* 3-4 year olds. The series prepares children to read and extend their vocabulary. In this book children can develop and practise preparatory skills for reading as well as realise God's giving character in creation.

BIBLE REFERENCES

All Bible references are in bold throughout and are as follows: p10 Genesis 1:24-25

ENCOURAGE CHILDREN TO:

* Talk about the illustrations and retell the story in their own words.
* Count the number of animals that they see when they go for a walk.
* Draw their own picture of their favourite animal.
* Memorise the Bible verse and its reference (see page 24).
* Sort their toy animals into sizes - big, medium and small.
* Talk about animals (with whom they are familiar) and where they live e.g. a kennel, hutch, basket etc.
* Ensure that the children know the meaning of all these words: *cheeky* (funny, trick loving, naughty); *gentle* (not rough, kind); *slimy* (slippery, sticky).

Carole Leah became a Christian at a youth camp when she was seventeen years old while reading a Gideon New Testament. She felt called to write these books so that young children would learn the truth about God while also developing their reading and vocabulary skills. Several people have worked alongside Carole as she wrote this material but she would like to especially dedicate these books to the memory of her dear friend Ruth Martin who gave so much support.

Joy, Todd and Daniel are in a house.
See what they are doing in this book!

The children are looking at a rabbit.
Joy and Daniel are looking after it for a friend.

Look for the frogs!

Can you find pictures of 10 frogs in this book?

Did you know that some frogs have stripes and
some have dots on them?

In the beginning

no animals lived on the earth.

God spoke and

made animals out of soil from the ground.

God gave the animals grass and

leafy plants to eat.

God created gentle animals

that were friendly.

God created animals that could dig.

He made animals that could slide into water and

swim.

He made ...**large and**

small... animals that could run and jump.

God **was pleased with what he saw**.

Now, Todd likes to see the strong horses and donkeys.

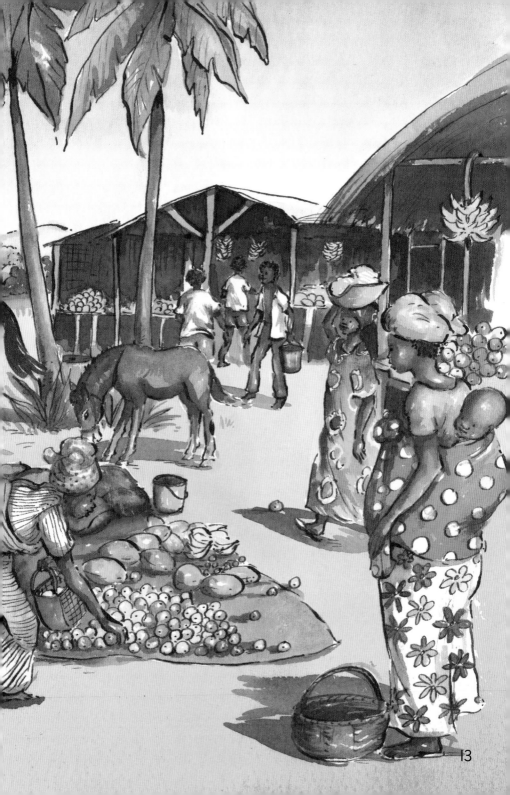

13

Daniel likes to see the big elephants and hippopotamuses.

Joy likes to look at the cheeky squirrels and slimy snails.

All the children like to find

many creepy-crawly creatures.

What funny noises some of them make!

Joy, Todd and Daniel have animals at home.

Joy has a cat called Tiddles.

Todd has a new puppy called Patch.

Daniel has an old goat called Billy.

Joy, Daniel and Todd are happy.

They love to look after God's animals.

They are kind and gentle to them.

We can enjoy God's animals, too!

God **gives animals their food...**

Psalm 147, verse 9